Aqua

PONIES+HORSES**BOOKS**

PONIES + HORSES BOOKS

Published by Ponies + Horses Books

Ponies + Horses Books (Scotland), 7b The Hidden
Lane, 1103 Argyle Street, Glasgow, G3 8ND

Ponies + Horses Books (Canada), Box 271, Stn C, Toronto, ON, M6J 3P4

www.poniesandhorsesbooks.com

First published by Ponies and Horses Books in 2015

I

Font: Gotham

Series Editor: Aefa Mulholland

Design: CraigDesign Studio

Series Copy Editor: Adrian Pasen

ISBN: 978-1-910631-45-4

MEMOIR

MEMOIR
ANTHOLOGY

6OF**1**

MEMOIR

CHICKEN
AND HEN

AEFA MULHOLLAND

For Joe

CHICKEN & HEN

When I was ten years old, my mum ran out to where I was riding my bike determinedly around the gardens in front of the house, her face flushed, her blue, paint-splotched smock flapping as she ran. My mum wasn't prone to loping across communal gardens in full sight of all the watchful neighbours, so I knew this must be something significant. As I screeched to a stop, she handed me an 8 by 10 photo of a small boy, with rumpled chestnut hair, a tentative smile and huge, brown, hopeful puppy eyes.

"This is your new brother," she said.

I dropped my bike and grabbed the photo, staring at the wee face.

"Is he really ours? To keep?"

She nodded, eyes brimming, and hugged me, both of

us still staring at the photo.

"He's called Brian."

She had just got the call—we had been approved to adopt this tiny, timid-looking toddler. I couldn't quite believe my luck. There I was, thinking that it'd be a good afternoon if I got to sneak across Hyndland Road to Chisholm's to get a few Cola Cubes or maybe a Tunnock's Teacake and here I was getting a wee brother. I was thrilled, but I was also taken by surprise. I had had no idea that my mum and dad had snuck out sibling-shopping on the sly, without mentioning what they were up to.

"Are you sure?" I pleaded. "Are you really sure this time?"

I'd taken it badly when the adoption of our last soon-to-be-new brother, Paddy, had fallen through two years earlier. And I'd found the process of being observed by social workers—as I attempted to appear wise, benevolent and older sisterly—stressful. I was already an older sister and up till then I had assumed that my duties revolved around attempting to persuade my wee sister to drink paint instead of milk, giving her regular bats round the head with a tennis racquet and issuing the very occasional invitation to dance to KC and the Sunshine Band with me and my best friend, Briony, when she least expected it. But what if there was more to it? What if there was some official Big Sister Checklist and I flunked it? The adoption home study visits felt like an audition for the part. And I was very poor at auditions. The combination of a crow-like croak and terminal stage fright had seen me denied even the role of Third Camel in the Notre Dame Primary musical last year and I'd been demoted to stagehand for this year's pop concert before I even opened my mouth. The social worker sessions made me anxious. And when I was anxious, I talked. A lot. About weird things.

I usually loved being the centre of attention—when there weren't camels or high-pitched musical numbers involved. Answering questions about myself was one of my all-time favourite activities. But these weren't questions or tests I could prepare for. My parents had told me just to be "myself," but did that really mean I should tell them about my plans to become the patron saint of cats, or that I was pretty sure I would eventually meet a talking horse or about the fortune I extracted from my siblings courtesy of the rigged one-armed bandit slot machine I made from a shoebox, a pencil and three thread bobbins?

During the home studies, I was acutely aware that my mum had been shuffled out of the room as Mel, the unsmiling social worker, asked careful questions, managing to remain expressionless throughout, regardless of how outlandish my answers got. Nobody ever told me if I'd got the questions right. What was the right answer to "Tell me about playtime," anyway? Maybe I shouldn't have answered "making cats dance" when Mel asked me what were my household chores. Maybe Orla had told him about the paint. Maybe my answers had taken Paddy away. This time around—having apparently passed the home study last time, despite my pronouncements—my parents had decided to keep this one under wraps until much later in the process, until Brian was a sure thing.

"We're definitely getting this one. You'll meet him on Saturday."

I looked at the tiny boy in the photograph with his huge, almost worried eyes and loved him immediately.

"It's still a secret, don't tell anyone yet," my mum called after me as I pedalled away, bellowing, "I'm getting a new wee brother! I'm getting a new wee brother!"

✱

My older sister Ciara died of leukemia when she was four, changing the family balance forever. Despite being so young when she died, I grew up acutely aware of her absence. A sadness sat at the table, with its empty seat where Ciara should have been. Our dynamics were forced to adjust. I became the middle of three. Mark became the eldest. Orla moved into a room of her own. My dad turned to Scotch. For a long time my mum lost God. Six years after Ciara died, my parents decided that we should adopt.

*

Orla had gone through several particularly demonic early years, so once my parents explained to me that adoption offered the option to acquire kids past the age when they were likely to bite you whenever you fell asleep, I immediately started campaigning to adopt any future siblings. Brian was almost three and so hopefully beyond the stage where he'd be likely to wreak vengeance on older siblings with his milk teeth.

In the years since she'd stopped gnawing my extremities, Orla had evolved into a studious child who dipped into random volumes of the *Encyclopedia Britannica* for fun by the age of five, while I—two years older—was still hooked on stories about magic trees, flatulent giants and anything that featured a talking animal. My older brother Mark was the precise number of years older that meant wee sisters weren't of much interest, so our contact was kept to a bare minimum, although he did sometimes appear with an unexpected present of a 45" single of something awesome like Survivor or Bucks Fizz for me and Briony to dance to. Mark and Orla went to the private, academic school in the city centre, while I went to the not particularly academic, nun-run one round the corner. A brand new brother, who I could go to school with and teach about important things like the possible whereabouts of talking horses and how much cats loved me, was just what I needed. I couldn't wait to have a new sibling.

*

When we were crammed into the stuffy living room in Brian's final foster home in Springburn, in the north of Glasgow, there he was; wearing a tiny cream polo neck tucked into the tiniest brown corduroy trousers, and tiny blue buckled shoes. He was two and three-quarters years old and was so small he looked as if he'd been shrunk in the wash. Compared to us, he seemed almost toy-sized.

Brian was absolutely minute for his age, while we, as a family, were very much not. I'd been the tallest in school when I still had two more years to go and, up till Brian appeared on the scene, I looked like I was going to be the shortest in the family; Mark was already heading for six foot and he was only 13. Overwhelmed by the sight of these five gargantuan creatures towering over him, Brian sensibly bolted and hid around the side of the overstuffed sofa, cowering just like Muffin the kitten did in the shoe cupboard, when we first got her as a consolation for Paddy disappearing from our weekends.

When everyone was distracted by Brian's grandmotherly foster mother arriving with tea and Kit Kats, I crept round the side of the couch, and said to him, in my polite, soft West End accent. "Hello, I'm Aefa, I'm your new sister."

"Speak up, hen, ah canny hear you!" he replied in the broadest, most guttural Glasgow accent.

While now I would caw with delight on hearing a two-foot-high child utter something so endearing as "hen"—long the traditional way of greeting a female Glaswegian—back then, aged 10 and a half, and used to people addressing each other as "dear," "darling" or in my Irish mum's case, "chicken," I was entirely taken aback. This was the first time I had ever been called "hen." Who was this creature? What language did he speak? How would I ever teach him how to win over a particularly curmudgeonly cat or have discussions with him about the best possible place to find loquacious equines if this was how he communicated?

I grew up in "The Gardens," 51 houses set round a central park in the west end of Glasgow. If you were going to invent a world filled with a cast of amusingly exaggerated middle class characters and then up the eccentric factor, you might find yourself describing The Gardens. Our neighbours included harpists, composers, artists, a reclusive Canadian photographer, a former Slovene presidential contender, various "Sirs" and "Ladies," plus several people who read the news on the B.B.C. In fact, it was pretty much obligatory to play for a symphony orchestra or present on the national broadcaster to live in The Gardens. And you'd probably have your membership of The Gardens Association revoked if you had never contemplated sending your children to private schools or been called to the bar—in the legal sense. I'd spent my entire life in this world. My dad owned a chain of newspapers. My mum was a stained glass artist. We were looked after by Nanny Smart and we definitely didn't say "hen." When you're ten years old, obsessed with talking animals and surrounded by other kids from the same sheltered background, a life like this seems entirely normal.

Back in Springburn, I tried again. Brian looked quizzical and said something incomprehensible. I asked the crucial question, " Do you like cats?" and he looked puzzled. He said something and I shrugged, bewildered. We didn't understand a single word the other said. I handed him a small bear I'd brought as a new brother bribe. He took it. I beamed at him. And he took my hand.

After he came to live with us, we always talked of when we "got" Brian, as if we'd fetched a new pet or we had slotted him in on the shopping list between a jumbo vat of margarine and the family pack of gammon steaks my mum cooked for us every Wednesday. We "got" Brian just after his third birthday. My mum fetched him. I don't now recall whether she picked up any gammon steaks or other groceries at the same time.

Brian arrived on our doorstep with the tiniest suitcase filled with the tiniest clothes, looking so small that I did actually try to see if my teddy bear's outfits fitted him. Some almost did.

*

Brian's character shone through right from the start. He was amused and amusing. He was generous and delighted with almost everything. He tried to think of compliments even when quite obviously underwhelmed. "I like tough potatoes," he piped at our granny one time over a dinner he found particularly hard to swallow. "This cake is music to my ears," he chirped at another. He was a happy wee thing who talked incessantly, even when underwater. He swam like a fish as soon as he met his first swimming pool, doing lengths with his mouth open. He was always running, always on the go, tripping constantly, laughing as he got up each time... until it occurred to someone that perhaps he should have his eyes tested. With the addition of thick prescription lenses, the falls stopped, but the laughter didn't.

Brian was a fascinating alien in our midst and we all adored him. As I'd hoped, Brian and I walked to school together, walked home together and danced on our beds to The Proclaimers and The Bangles after doing our homework. We did each other's hair—his spiked like a stegosaurus tail, mine up like a pineapple. We wrote each other stories about magic trees, talking horses and how great cats were. And about the things he loved—dogs, swimming and causing mischief.

He was idolized at school, befriending all the underdogs, the shy kids, the boy with severe Down Syndrome, the wee girl who was picked on. People couldn't get over how sweet and charming this tiny, talkative child was. Kids and adults flocked around him.

I sat opposite Brian at the dinner table, the empty seat now filled. When our more academically inclined siblings conversed with my parents on subjects such as an obscure philosophical twist in Huysmans' À *Rebours* or the deteriorating political situation in Uganda, Brian and I would occupy ourselves with intellectual pursuits such as making faces at each other over our plates or writing notes to each other with stalks of asparagus. At the point when I was on the verge of descending into inappropriate giggles, I'd bite my lip and try to focus on reading the titles of the books on the shelves behind Brian's head. One book always caught my eye. It was called *Our Illustrious Forebears*. Both Brian and I were puzzled and disappointed when we finally took the book off the shelf, crowded over it and found not one single illustration of a bear.

But there were times he didn't laugh. For our first newly expanded family holiday, we went to the island of Arran, off the west coast, where Brian cried, terrified of the vast monster that crept up behind him in a field, so huge compared to his tiny dimensions.

"It's just a sheep, chicken," my mum reassured him.

"Sheeps are a lot bigger than they look in books," he sniffed.

My dad whisked him up in his arms and promised he would always defend him from sheeps.

Maybe Brian had never seen a sheep before. Maybe he'd never even been out of Glasgow until then. Social workers can tell you headlines, but there's an awful lot about an adopted child's past that stays under the surface. Other things that stopped Brian's sudden, delighted laugh and made him cower and cry were parties and the sight of suitcases.

What I didn't know back then, but my parents did, was what Brian's life had been like before he arrived on our doorstep, me bowled over by the perfect toy doll smallness of him. I didn't know that coming to us was his tenth move in three years, or that there had been a party thrown for him as he left each foster home, followed by a packed suitcase, the sign of another departure. I didn't know about the hospitalizations, skull fractures and beatings he'd suffered through during the first twenty-four months of his life. I didn't know he'd been given up by his adoring teenaged mum when he was just two or that she came to see him in every foster home, every single day, until the afternoon he came to live with us. I didn't know then that such a tiny perfect creature could have been through so much heartbreak.

As he settled in and grew, my mum tried to correct

his pronunciation, so he'd blend in with the kids in the area. "It's not 'mulk,' it's 'milk,'" she told him—and then we all tried to keep straight faces when Brian, tired of the teatime lesson, pouted and said, "I'm in a silk."

His vocab was extensive and inventive, He read constantly, voraciously. While all of us had a love of books in common, in other areas, we were an unlikely set. Mark, Orla and I were far taller than all other kids in the neighbourhood, while Brian was much smaller. We looked alike—people often couldn't tell "the girls" apart— Brian was a different build entirely. We all adored cats; Brian hugged every dog he met. We obediently went to super-Catholic schools, slunk into weekly Confession and were trooped down the aisle for Communion every Sunday at St. Peter's of Partick; meanwhile Brian was determined to support Rangers, the Protestant football team. He wore the blue Rangers strip to Mass, much to the consternation of many a wee Glasgow Catholic lady. While we excelled at English, music and art, Brian quickly won places on Glasgow's sports teams, from swimming to rugby to karate. We were opposites in many ways, but he was a perfect fit... or, rather, the family nestled into a new shape around him.

Add any new human to a family and that unit becomes a different thing. Take a tried and tested recipe and throw in something completely unknown—an ingredient from another food group—and you end up with a very different cake. I remember, at the time, thinking of us in recipe terms, with him as the garnish, like a smatter of Smarties on top. But it didn't turn out that way. Regardless when they're added to the mix, add a new member to a family and they're there, right through the batter, they're in every mouthful. Brian made us something new entirely.

The ten-year-old me expected it would take a while for Brian to adapt to Mulholland Family ways. That's not how it worked, of course. Where we thought he'd learn our language and our ways, we adapted to his. It was his expressions that became family catchphrases, his unique take on life that made us think and rethink things. "Mission accomplicated," he'd say with a rueful grin, when things didn't go quite his way. And ever since he referred to one of my mum's creations as her "mistresspiece," that's what we called her artworks. "Will you promise to miss me?" he asked my parents one night as they went out. How could they not?

Brian grew up, stocky and strong. He remained kind, funny and generous. I never managed to persuade him that cats were better than dogs. He never missed an opportunity to tell me that he loved me.

Brian was responsible for myriad Mulholland family firsts; he was the first to have a dog, the first to swim for Glasgow, the first to take up martial arts, the first to support Rangers, the first—and only one of us—to have a kid, the first to have a criminal record.

When he turned 18, he was given the photo album his birth mum had left for him, filled with photos of the two of them, of his cousin, of his grandparents, of him standing on the grey streets he'd lived on during his first two years—and, at the back, there was a letter explaining why she had decided he was better off living with us and not her.

The next day he said to me, "Don't tell the parents. I want to try and find her. Will you come with me?"

We headed east. There was an Old Firm football match that day, Celtic were playing Rangers, crowds in green or blue spilling out of every street end as we inched through town. The taxi driver dropped us off at a dejected, pot-holed street corner, but wouldn't take us any further into the neighbourhood of rundown houses where Brian's birth mum had written the letter.

Most windows on the street's dejected, damp, five- and six-storey buildings were boarded up. We found the address and went into the communal close, up the stairs, the stench of mould hitting hard as we climbed. Half of the flat doors we passed were sealed with metal grates, like they had been condemned. We reached the top flat where she used to live, her door, once Brian's door. It was closed over with steel, too. She'd gone. Maybe recently. Maybe 15 years ago. It rained icy rain all the way home. The bus was hot, stuffy, falsely bright. It crawled through traffic all the way back to the West End.

"I just wanted someone of my own," Brian said quietly.

Back on the other side of town, away from all the football mayhem, Mum was waiting for us on the doorstep, as if she'd known he'd need her, "Ah, there you are," she said, as he trudged up the front steps. She hugged him tightly as he hugged her back.

"I've got you, chicken," she said.

"You have," he said.

*

After that, there were years of ups and downs. Always one to see opportunity where no one else did, Brian went through a slew of daft schemes, like the time he decided to set up a cigarette smuggling business from the Czech Republic to the U.K.

"There's hardly any competition," he exclaimed, "Just the Russian mafia…"

Increasingly, there were more downs. There were missed buses, missed chances, lost phones, lost jobs, lost wallets. Late night and early morning emergency phone calls.

I tried to fish him out of one situation, but he'd be back in another the following week. Brian would tell me sheepishly about the consequences of the latest hurdle, his latest arrest. Regardless what he was going through, he never lost hope. And no matter how bad things got, he would still try to cheer me up. He sent texts; "You still number one chick!," "Love Young Brother in Glasgow Jungle," "I love you and miss you and think about you all the time."

We tried, Mark, Orla, our parents and I. but things got darker and darker. Arrests, convictions, attacks. Broken legs, break-ins, burnt out cars. The wrong side of the wrong people. One time, eighty-seven stitches, twenty-seven metal staples in his head, four pints of lost blood. Another time, half a brick, left for dead. The next, a coma for three days. We got to fear the phone ringing. We steeled ourselves to expect the worst.

*

On the New Year's Day that he turned twenty-five, Brian phoned, his voice cracking with joy, to tell me his son, Wee Joe, had been born that morning. Things were turning around for him.

"I got lost in the Glasgow Jungle," he said. "But I've got Joe now."

He trained and became a lifeguard. He worked with disabled kids, in hospitals and old folks' homes. He tried so hard to be there for Wee Joe. He tried so hard to stay clean.

A year and a half after Joe was born, he called me from another rehab or another hostel or another halfway house somewhere in the north of England.

He joked, "Speak up, hen, I canny hear you," then cheerfully said, "I have to go before someone puts a razor blade in my soup."

"Och, chicken," I said.

Brian's gone ten years now, found dead of a heroin overdose, aged just 26. Life is quieter, calmer, emptier and far, far less colourful without him.

Brian shook up everything in the family that became his—both as an utterly charming wee boy and as a hilarious, always hopeful adult. We became something else, with Brian added to us. Something richer, fuller, with a more uneven, but far more interesting texture. We are all different people for having that tiny wee three-year-old become part of us.

The teenage Brian was the first to say, "I love you," something known, but never before uttered in our often careful, buttoned up family. Brian was always generous with love.

*

I'm lucky to have had Brian in my life for twenty-three wild, full, colourful years.

I'm lucky that Brian's wee boy, Joe, is a huge part of my life. Now he and I do each other's hair—blue hair mascara streaks for him and a pineapple do for me—and we breakdance to Dolly Parton and Kid Rock in the playroom in the house his dad grew up in.

I'm lucky that the last thing that Brian and I said to each other was "I love you."

Of course, Brian said it first.

PONIES**+**HORSES**BOOKS**

ABOUT

Aefa Mulholland, is an award-winning travel and food writer. Born in Glasgow, Scotland, she now divides her time between Toronto and Glasgow. Aefa has worked with national broadcasters in the U.K., Ireland and Canada, and with a plethora of publications from The Miami Herald to The Irish Times. She has been published or broadcast on four continents, writing or presenting on subjects from mule racing in Montana to the hazards of bingo in Glasgow to partying with The Pixies in Dublin. Her work has won a Northern Lights Award for Excellence in Travel Writing and an Irish Film Board award. Other things that Aefa has won include a national poetry competition (aged 6) for a heartfelt poem about a dead deer, £3 betting on a mouse race in North Tipperary and $12 in the New York State Lottery.

She writes offbeat hotel reviews and destination guides for Angry Sea Turtles and is working on a documentary on career options for seahorses. She is the author of full-length travel memoir, The Scottish Ambassador, published by P+H Books in August 2015.

www.aefamulholland.com

POP

TANIA KATAN

POP

TANIA KATAN

In *Pop*, **Tania Katan** invites us along for the ride as she and her pop crash a company picnic, do yoga by osmosis and finally face a potentially life-changing diagnosis together as she learns to be proud of her unpredictable, unorthodox and formerly unreliable dad.

ACHING
TO BE

ANDREW J. FITT

ACHING TO BE

ANDREW J. FITT

A boy with Cerebral Palsy dreams of living his own life in **Andrew J. Fitt's** honest *Aching To Be.* Determined not to let a few unfortunate seconds at birth stop him from being the man he wants to be, Andrew learns to talk, to type and to walk, as he grows into a determined young man, hell-bent on living life on his own terms.

THE
AWKWARD
STAGE

SOPHIA BLACKWELL

THE AWKWARD STAGE

SOPHIA BLACKWELL

In **Sophia Blackwell's** *The Awkward Stage*, an English teenager finds herself in the wrong time, the wrong town and the wrong body. Surviving adolescence in her humdrum home town with the help of musicals, magazine problem pages and an enigmatic schoolmate, she dreams of becoming a Broadway star.

WHOOSH

HILLARY SAVOIE

WHOOSH

HILLARY SAVOIE

A baby's heart stops beating and a mother struggles to come to terms with the unrecognizable version of life she finds on the other side of her daughter's cardiac arrest in **Hillary Savoie's** powerful and poignant *Whoosh*.

CHICKEN AND HEN

AEFA MULHOLLAND

CHICKEN AND HEN

AEFA MULHOLLAND

Aefa Mulholland recounts the story of her family's adoption of a tiny, talkative three-year-old from the other side of town, from his first words to her to his final goodbye, in the heartwarming and heartbreaking *Chicken & Hen*.

BLUE BABY ORANGE TANK

TRACY CRAIG

BLUE BABY ORANGE TANK

TRACY CRAIG

Tracy Craig takes us back to her childhood on the tropical island of Trinidad in *Blue Baby Orange Tank*. Born with a hole in her heart, Tracy tells of her oxygen-deprived early years and the sometimes unlikely strategies her eccentric parents employed in order to keep her alive until she was old enough to have open-heart surgery.

TRAVEL

GERALDINE
DERUITER

AEFA
MULHOLLAND

CARLA
WILSON

MATTHEW
LINK

HILLARY
SAVOIE

DENNIS
HENSLEY

TRAVEL 6 of 1

Available as individual, standalone books or as an anthology, **TRAVEL 6 of 1**, the first series of short travel essays from P+H Books, contains stories that stretch right from the moment of birth to the sometimes surprisingly colourful business of death. There are tales of arrivals and departures, ships that have sailed and ships that have come in. There are stories of festivities perched on the brink of a war zone, on the brim of the Mediterranean and on the banks of the Mississippi.

Our authors have contributed tales of Accra, Ghana; Valencia, Spain; Memphis, Tennessee; Damascus, Syria; plus a mixtape of port calls and cruise jobs from Hong Kong to Alaska through the Panama Canal and on to the Caribbean; and a journey that perhaps travels further than any of the others, yet doesn't leave Boston, Massachusetts.

TRAVEL

CHILDHOOD

TANIA
KATAN

ANDREW J.
FITT

SOPHIA
BLACKWELL

HILLARY
SAVOIE

AEFA
MULHOLLAND

TRACY
CRAIG

MEMOIR 6 of 1

Available as individual, standalone books or as an anthology, **MEMOIR 6 of 1**, the first collection of short memoirs from P+H Books, takes a look at childhood from all directions. The funny and moving series of stories features unconventional fathers, unexpected kids, challenging childhoods and plenty of triumph over adversity, expectation, small city limitations and potato sack races.

MEMOIR

THE SCOTTISH AMBASSADOR

Learning How To Be Scottish in America

66 *Very funny and entertaining... Will amuse readers of every stripe.* 99
ALASDAIR GRAY

AEFA MULHOLLAND

THE SCOTTISH AMBASSADOR
LEARNING HOW TO BE SCOTTISH IN AMERICA

AEFA MULHOLLAND

Ex-pat Scot Aefa Mulholland travels around the U.S.,
persuading bemused Americans to teach her how to
be a better Scot. From learning how to do Scottish
Country Dancing in Honolulu to attempting golf
for the first time on a rattlesnake-infested desert
sand golf course in a trailer park in Arizona and
learning how to play the bagpipes in New Orleans,
she learns about what it means to be Scottish,
what it means to be Scottish-American and what it
means to be at home such a long way from home.

PONIESANDHORSESBOOKS.COM

PONIES+HORSES**BOOKS**

the "Mostly" true **Adventures Of Jim Craig:**

SAILBOATS, DRAGONS & GIRAFFES

Written & Illustrated by Tracy Craig

THE MOSTLY TRUE ADVENTURES OF JIM CRAIG: SAILBOATS, DRAGONS & GIRAFFES

TRACY CRAIG

A beautifully illustrated story of adventure, polka-dotted dragons, talking onions and tap-dancing sharks, The Mostly True Adventures of Jim Craig: Sailboats, Dragons & Giraffes, follows the adventures of the indomitable Jim as he sails across the Atlantic from England to Trinidad and Tobago.

Aimed at kids from age 3 to 8 (but sure to be appreciated by readers of all ages), Sailboats, Dragons & Giraffes is out now and is the first in a series of quirky adventure/travel picture books about the feisty Jim, crammed with character, ninja starfish and busy business elks. Visit P+H online to find out more.

PONIESANDHORSESBOOKS.COM

Lightning Source UK Ltd.
Milton Keynes UK
UKOW06f0716191115

263055UK00006B/89/P